A BOOT UP

BLACKMORE VALE

Rodney Legg

First published in Great Britain in 2011

Copyright text and photographs © 2011 Rodney Legg

British Library Cataloguing-in-Publication Data
A CIP record for this title is available from the British Library

ISBN 978 0 85710 022 1

PiXZ Books
Halsgrove House, Ryelands Industrial Estate,
Bagley Road, Wellington, Somerset TA21 9PZ
Tel: 01823 653777
Fax: 01823 216796
email: sales@halsgrove.com

An imprint of Halstar Ltd, part of the Halsgrove group of companies
Information on all Halsgrove titles is available at: www.halsgrove.com

Printed and bound in China by Toppan Leefung Printing Ltd

Contents

Blackmore Vale

How to use this book

The Area

The name of the Blackmore Vale sums up its historic character but in the time of Henry III this royal hunting ground - a 'forest' for sport rather than silviculture - had a romantic moniker, Vale of the White Hart. The legend of King's Stag is that the King spared the life of an albino female deer which he had hunted near Lydlinch. The monarch was then enraged to hear that his forest bailiff had killed the beast beside the bridge over the River Lydden. Henry punished local people by imposition of a tax which became known as white hart silver.

The spelling of the Blackmore Vale is still given as 'Blackmoor' by the Ordnance Survey but its alternative spelling is now paramount thanks to the popularity of the *Blackmore Vale Magazine* as the principal local organ. This undulating landscape of the River Stour and its main tributaries forms the heart of northern Dorset, below the escarpments of the Dorset Downs to the south and Cranborne Chase to the east.

The Routes

All routes are circular - meaning they bring you back to the starting point - and are of moderate length. They vary from **four to eight** miles and are graded from one to three boots - from easy to the more challenging. They are ideal for families or groups of friends looking for an afternoon in glorious historic countryside or for a more leisurely walk with a suitable pause at a pub or refreshment spot en route. None of the terrain is push-chair friendly, so back-pack the toddler. Starting points are given with map references and postcodes, because the latter are necessary for some car-borne navigation systems, including that used by an ambulance crew who told me they were 15 minutes late in arriving at an emergency because no postcode was given.

Direction details specify compass points which, clockwise, are N (north), NNE (north-northeast), NE (north-east), ENE (east-northeast), E (east), ESE (east-southeast), SE (south-east),

SSE (south-southeast), S (south), SSW (south-southwest), SW (south-west), WSW (west-southwest), W (west), WNW (west-northwest), NW (north-west) and NNW (north-north-west). The general direction can be assumed to remain the same until another compass point is given. Carry a compass to confirm the direction and secateurs for getting through rampant vegetation around stiles.

Routes are along public rights of way or across access land. Both categories may be subject to change or diversion. Remember that conditions under foot will vary greatly according to the season and the weather. Flash-floods are a local speciality. I nearly lost my car a short distance from the spot where a driver was being washed to

his death from the ford beside the packhorse bridge at Fifehead Neville. That village is also remembered for an unfortunate incident in which a lady was trampled to death when cattle reacted badly to a yapping dog.

Parking spaces are specified on the assumption that many walkers will arrive by car or bicycle. Where public transport is mentioned, there were options currently available, but check these with the provider before setting off and always make sure you also know the time of the last bus or train.

The Maps

Though we give a self-contained pot-ted description of each walk you may need a map or global positioning system to find its parking point. Our

sketch maps can only be a rough guide. A detailed map will prove use-ful if you stray away from the route or are forced to cut the walk short. Remember that practical difficulties on the day may range from heat exhaus-tion to flood water.

The Blackmore Vale spreads across three large-scale sheets of the Ordnance Survey. The northern and central parts currently appear on two sides of Explorer Map 129 (Yeovil & Sherborne). Southern and western areas are on the east side of Explorer Map 117 (Cerne Abbas & Bere Regis). The eastern extremity runs down the side of Explorer Map 118 (Shaftesbury & Cranborne Chase). For availability access www.ordnancesurvey.co.uk/leisure.

Key to Symbols Used

Level of difficulty:

Easy 🍂

Fair 🍂 🍂

More challenging 🍂 🍂 🍂

Map symbols:

🚗 Park & start

— Road

- - - Track

----- Footpath

■ Building / Town

+ Church

🍺 Pub

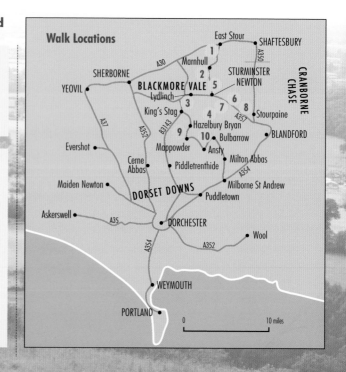

Walk Locations

East Stour

SHAFTESBURY

A30 Marnhull

1

2

SHERBORNE 5 STURMINSTER NEWTON

YEOVIL BLACKMORE VALE

Lydlinch

3 7 6 8

King's Stag 4 Stourpaine

9 Hazelbury Bryan

10 Bulbarrow BLANDFORD

Evershot Mappowder Ansty

Cerne Abbas Piddletrenthide Milton Abbas

Maiden Newton Milborne St Andrew

DORSET DOWNS Puddletown

Askerswell A35 DORCHESTER

Wool

A352

WEYMOUTH

PORTLAND

CRANBORNE CHASE

0 10 miles

1 Stour Provost and Fifehead Magdalen

A 4-mile circuit of the River Stour and its northern meadows

Stour Provost village is a delightful thatched cul-de-sac between meanderings of the upper Stour.

The watery theme is bolstered by lakes and trout pools which are linked by lengths of riverside walking. Herons and moorhen are common and otter spraints present. The main road from Henstridge to Shaftesbury is crossed beside the Ship Inn in West Stour village. With the noteworthy exception of the Ship Inn, still very much on the menu, this is an area where every other building seems to carry the 'Old' epithet. There has been a passing of the little shops along with a whole way of life. A typical 'closed' village lies along the

Level: 🐾 🐾
Length: 4 miles
Terrain: Liable to be muddy for much of the year and under water at times when rainfall is in season.
Park and Start: Towards the top end of the village street in Stour Provost, in the vicinity of Provost House.
Start ref.: NT 894280
Postcode: SP8 5SA
Public transport: Buses from Sturminster Newton and Shaftesbury.
Websites: www.shipinn-dorset.com
www.ukvillages.co.uk

lanes at Fifehead Magdalen, adjoining meadows towards Marnhull. The 'Old Mill' here has vanished but Stour Provost Mill is intact.

Map labels: West Stour, 4, nsend arm, 5, 3, 6, Riverdale Farm, head dalen, 12, 2, 7, Mill, 1 Stour Provost, 8, 11, River Stour, Trill Bridge, 10, thy Cottage, 9, 500m

St Michael's church

 Set off uphill to the crossroads and turn left (E) beside **Antles Farm**, away from Pantiles and Corner Cottage. Turn left (N) in 50 metres, after **St Michael's Cottage**, into the churchyard. Pass to the left of **St Michael's church**, downhill to the other corner in 100 metres, and turn left (W) into a grassy path for 50 metres.

 Turn right (N) in **The Street**, down from **Brookside**

Stour Provost

Cottage and your car, to pass the last thatch at **Mundy's Cottage**. The asphalt ends at **Riverdale Farm** in 350 metres. Pedestrians fork to the right of the farm and then turn left (N), along the green lane beside the buildings, which are to your left. In 100 metres we turn left through the metal gate into the second meadow, after the trout ponds.

 Bear right (NW) diagonally towards the village strung out along the hill. Cross a stream beside the willows in the corner of the next field in 350 metres. Proceed to the **River Stour** in 175 metres. Keep the river to your right and cross a footbridge in 250 metres. Continue straight ahead, uphill, into **West Stour** in 400 metres. Towards the

Missionary Mildred Cable (1878-1952), who retired to Willow Cottage in Stour Row, was the first western woman to cross the Gobi Desert.

top, in 250 metres, cross into the next field to the right. Emerge in 150 metres on opposite **The Ship** coaching inn which dates from 1750.

 Turn left (SW), uphill along the pavement beside the

A30 for 200 metres, passing **Spring Cottage** and **Fieldgate Cottage**. The pavement comes to an abrupt end. Walk towards the oncoming traffic for 100 metres to thatched **Little Ashley**. Cross with care from the sloping roadside verge, to a track opposite the

cottage, beside **Pickwicks** (before Townsend Farm).

 Follow the right-hand hedge (S) for the length of the garden. Cross the stile in 50 metres and continue straight ahead across

Water meadows

The Ship Inn

Fifehead Magdalen, to historian John Hutchins, was 'as pleasant a spot as any in the county of Dorset'.

the field. Keep straight on, across stiles, at the next three hedgerows. From the top of the hill, beneath the horse chestnuts in 500 metres, cross the first stile and then bear left to another stile in 10 metres.

6 Bear right (SSE), towards the pair of oak trees, to a stile in the fence on the other side of the pasture in 200 metres. Continue straight ahead, between the oaks and a cedar, to skirt the ha-ha of **Fifehead Manor** in 175 metres. Keep the brick and stone wall to your right for 150 metres. Its Georgian house was demolished in 1964.

7 Turn right (NW) on reaching the road, uphill into **Fifehead Magdalen**, to pass **St Mary Magdalene church** in 75 metres. Walk along the pavement, to the **Old Post Office**, just before the telephone box in 200 metres.

8 Turn left (S), across the road, along a public path beside the

Geese in a downpour

Fifehead Magdalen

yew tree alongside the 1860-dated **Old School House**. Keep straight ahead, for 1,200 metres, across arable fields to the River Stour, which is to your left at first, and cross it at a foot-bridge in 200 metres. This is near the site of the **Old Mill**. Continue

straight ahead. Cross a stile and keep to the left of **Withy Cottage** and **Spring Cottage** in 100 metres.

9 On reaching the end of the public road, at the gate, we turn immediately left (NE) and keep

Fifehead Magdalen House, now one of Dorset's lost country mansions, was demolished in 1964.

the river to our left for the remainder of the walk. Head for molehill-shaped Duncliffe Hill. Cross stiles. The final one is in the hedgerow after and between two lakes in 1,000 metres.

10 Turn left (NW) at the road (ignoring the path opposite because we are taking a much more picturesque route to Stour Provost). Go down the road for 120 metres. Then turn right (N) immediately before **Trill Bridge**. Again keep the river to your left. In 150 metres the

Wisteria at Fifehead

Stour Provost Mill

path bears left and Fifehead Magdalen is now the village in front of us.

(11) In a further 300 metres, after the third stile, bear right (NE) away from both the river and Fifehead village. Our target is the lower end of Stour Provost. Cross the pasture and then go through the gap in the hedge

to the left of the lower house in 500 metres. Keep to the left of the first part of **Meads Farm** and then turn right, into it, to pass above the left-hand barns.

(12) On reaching the asphalt road in 100 metres, we turn left (N), across the pasture, to see **Stour Provost Mill** and its 1886-dated

wheel. Go through the gate immediately to the left of the wheel-house. Then turn left through a smaller gate, on the other side of the mill-stream, in 8 metres. Once again keep the river to the left. Proceed upstream for 50 metres to a stile. Bear right (ENE), uphill across the pasture, and keep the next group of buildings to your left in 150 metres. The track becomes a lane, for 100 metres, into the middle of the village. Turn right (S) to return to your car.

2 **Marnhull and Hinton St Mary**

*A 7-mile circuit of undulating landscape
close to the river*

Flatter countryside widens after Marnhull where the Stour begins to justify its river status by gathering the Cale from Wincanton and the Lydden from the Lydlinch direction. Coming from the heart of the Blackmore Vale, the Lydden tributary carries a substantial winter flow, into a broad confluence below King's Mill Bridge. Marnhull village comprises multiple lanes and even more public paths. At times there is too much of a good thing with a confusion of options. The next village downstream, at Hinton St Mary, has a very different character. Its historic parts cluster beside an aristocratic Manor House. Later additions line each side of the turnpike road that passes through. There is no visible sign of its great treasure - a

Map labels:

Marnhull
Crown Hotel
Primary School
Pope's Farm
New Street
Common Lane
Eastwell Lane
Sewage Works
Yardgrove Farm
ng's ill
Cutt Mill
Joyce's Coppice
Stearts Lane
White Horse Inn
Hinton St Mary
Home Farm
River Stour
River ydden
Wood Lane
Manor House
500 m
1 2 3 4 5 6 7 8 9 10 11 12

Level: 🥾 🥾
Length: 7 miles
Terrain: Low hills, arable fields and meadows
Park & start: In New Street, opposite Senior's Farm and the Primary School, at Marnhull.
Start ref.: ST 780 187
Postcode: DT10 1PZ
Public transport: Buses from Sturminster Newton and Shaftesbury.
Websites: www.hintonstmary.com
www.marnhullmessenger.org.uki

Roman villa dating from 350 AD - which had a fine mosaic floor. Its centrepiece, with a roundel featuring the head of Christ, is now displayed in the British Museum.

Set off (E) to **St Gregory's church** in 200 metres. Proceed straight ahead at the cross-roads, along **Crown Road**, to the **Crown Hotel** in 125 metres. Immediately after it, opposite the entrance to **The Barn**, turn right (S) and pass between the outer barns of **Church Farm** to the hedgerow on the other side in 100 metres. To the right of this you go through a metal gate. Walk straight ahead and follow

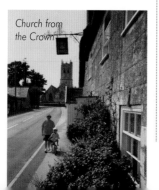

Church from the Crown

Crown Hotel

the right-hand hedge, crossing the fence by a cattle-trough in 100 metres, down into the far centre corner of the pasture in 250 metres.

Turn left (SE) through a gate, 50 metres from the corner, and bear right across the arable field to a gate to the right of a small wood in 175 metres. Bear left, keeping the wood to the left, to the gate on the other side in 125 metres. Turn right

(S) along the concrete farm road, up to **Eastwell Lane**, in 200 metres.

Turn right (W), up the road, for 150 metres. Turn left (S) through the second of the two gates. Follow the hedgerow, keeping it to your left, to double stiles and a foot-bridge at the end of the field in 400 metres. Continue straight ahead across the track with the **Sewage Works** to your left, for 100 metres,

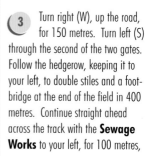

The stained glass east window in St Gregory's church, to Victorian rector Robert Bruce Kennard, who died in 1895, is one of the last pieces of work by Sir Edward Burne-Jones (1833-98).

and then bear right from the corner, into the field and towards a hilltop wood on the other side of the valley. En route we cross a stile and ditch at the hedgerow in the dip in 200 metres.

(4) On reaching the trees, in a further 200 metres, follow the path straight ahead. This is

Lakes Plantation. The path bends right and then left to exit from the wood in 600 metres. Follow the track up the incline into **Hinton St Mary** in 200 metres.

(5) Turn left (SE) along **Veals Lane**, passing **Haye Cottage**, to the junction with **Steart Lane** in 150 metres. Turn left (NE)

Village blacksmith William White discovered the remarkable Romano-Christian mosaic at Hinton St Mary in 1964.

Manor gates

Hinton St Mary Manor House

St Mary's church

and pass **Bartlett's Depot** in 150 metres. After the machinery compound, in a further 100 metres, turn right (S) along the drive at the slight bend in the road. Go down into the dip and up to a cross-roads, in 300 metres, at **Home Farm**.

(6) Turn right (E) up **Ridgeway Lane**. Pass the **Manor House** home of the Pitt-Rivers family and follow the road round to **St Mary's church** in 400 metres. Proceed to the cross-roads beside the **White Horse** in 100 metres. Turn

left (SE), passing the site of the Roman villa, down to the main road in 175 metres. Cross this into **Wood Lane**. Pass **Wood Lane Cottage** and the farm entrance in 400 metres. Continue straight ahead for a further 100 metres.

(7) Turn right (NW) into the bridleway. Turn left (SW) in 175 metres and then bear right (W) in 100 metres, to go down and around the corner of the field. Follow its left-hand fence (N) to the next

White Horse Inn

Lydden-Stour confluence

corner in 500 metres. The river valley opens out to the left. Go through a bridleway gate and continue straight ahead into **Joyce's Coppice**. Keep its wooded slopes to your left. In 300 metres the path dips down to a hunting gate.

 Here you have the option of a diversion, down the road for

150 metres, to the **River Stour** at **Cutt Mill** (currently in limbo after being gutted by fire). The H. E. Bates novel *Set Fair the Wind for France* was filmed here in 1942. Our onward route, however, is the other way. Turn right (NE), uphill, for 150 metres. Then turn left (NW), across the stile into the field, and follow the hedgerow to the corner in 300 metres. Turn right (NE), across the ditch, into the next field and keep its hedgerow to your left for 100 metres. Then turn left (N), crossing the stiles, straight ahead into the field. Continue straight ahead, following the fence in 200 metres and then crossing a stile, to a pond in a further 250 metres.

Bear left (NW) in the following field, down to a track

which leads to **Yardgrove Farm** in 200 metres. Go through a gate and turn left to exit on to the asphalt lane. Keep straight ahead along it, passing the farmhouse to the right, to the junction in 250 metres.

10 Turn left (SW) down **Cox Hill** to the confluence of the Lydden and Stour, at **King's Mill**, in 800 metres. Turn right (N) between the house and bridge. Follow the drive to the older barn to the left of the house and cross the fence beside them. The public path skirts farmyard

King's Mill

buildings (NE) and follows the power cables in 250 metres. Go through the iron gate on the other side of the field in 200 metres. Walk straight across to the gate to the left of the 1866-dated gabled house in 150 metres.

11 Turn left (NNW) along **Common Lane** for 250 metres. Turn right (NE) across the culverted section of ditch, over the stile, for 50 metres. After the double-hedged path we follow the right-hand hedgerow up the hill. Go through the gate in 150 metres and bear left. Aim for the cluster of tiled buildings on the brow of the hill in 300 metres. This is **Pope's Farm** with the thatch to the right being **Pope's Cottage**.

12 Leave the field at the gate and turn right for 15 metres. Turn left at the junction, for 20 metres, and then turn right into the field. Bear left to walk diagonally across it. Cross the fence in the far corner and

Marnhull's 'smokers' epitaph' is to John Warren who died at the age of 94 in 1752: 'Here under this stone lie Ruth and old John who smoked all his life, as did his wife.'

keep the hedgerow to your left as you approach the fir trees beside the bungalow in 350 metres. Descend steps to the road. Turn right to return to **New Street** in 750 metres.

Stour at Marnhull

3 **Lydlinch and Stock Gaylard**

A 5-mile circuit of the central flat-lands with an aristocratic deer-herd

Lydlinch is at the low-lying heart of the Blackmore Vale where the tributaries of the Caundle Brook and the River Lydden merge before emptying in the River Stour. It is also the meeting place of the two main roads that cross the flat-lands, being the A357 from Blandford to Wincanton, and the A3030 from Sherborne. They meet in a superb remnant of mediaeval open landscape at Lydlinch Common where nightingales breed in the blackthorn scrub and rare marsh fritillary butterflies enliven wide drifts of coarse grass. Stock Gaylard is a Queen Anne house in an 80-acre deer park which has the largest herd of fallow deer in Dorset. Its church has a crusader figure to its supposed founder of 750 years ago, and a

Level: 🍃 🍃
Length: 5 miles
Terrain: Flat but muddy.
Park & start: Turn off the A357 in Lydlinch village, into Holebrook Lane, and park beside the common on the right-hand side in 150 metres.
Start ref.: ST 743 135
Postcode: DT10 2JA
Public transport: Buses from Blandford to Sherborne.
Websites: www.stockgaylard.com
www.visionofbritain.org.uk

life-size bronze by Henry Pegram to a warrior of the Great War, Captain Harry Farr Yeatman, who fell in sight of Jerusalem in 1917.

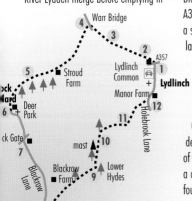

1 Set off (N) towards the main road. Pass the **Old School** and **Coronation Oak** (for Edward VII in 1902) in the grassy corner of **Lydlinch Common** in 150 metres. Cross the A357, to the opening on the other side, between **The Croft** and a shed supported on staddle stones. Go through the gate in front of you and turn left (WNW) in the field in 50 metres, to follow the hedge downhill to the pastures below **Vale Farm** in 200 metres.

2 Bear right in the next field, and cross the stile to the right of railings, on the other side in 75 metres. Then follow the left-hand

'Lydlinch bells be good vor sound, an' liked by all the neighbours round,' to quote dialect verse published in 1859 by parson-poet William Barnes.

hedge and exit at the opening in 250 metres. Turn right (NW) on the other side, with a pond to your left, walk directly across the field to the opening on the other side in 150 metres. Go over two stiles and take care when crossing the ditch.

3 Bear right across this field to the remains of a stone bridge at the next ditch in 150 metres. Turn right on the other side and go through the opening into the next field in 100

Vintage outing to Coronation Oak

The church at Stock Gaylard, rebuilt in 1885, stands on an ancient site.

metres. Bear left, diagonally, to a gate just left of **Warr Bridge** in 300 metres. **Caundle Brook** and Waterloo Lane turnpike tollhouse is to the right.

(4) Cross the main road to the black Y-gate that is the emblem of Yeatman Estate. Bear left (SW) across this field, diagonally, to the gate in the far corner in 400 metres. Cross the next field to the gate beside the water-trough in the top right-hand corner 200 in metres. Bear right (SW) to the right-hand side of **Stroud Farm**. Continue straight

Stock Gaylard church

ahead across the track, to the right of the farm in 300 metres, and proceed to the left-hand end of the right-hand wood in a further 200 metres.

(5) Pass **Stock Gaylard Park** for 150 metres. It is renowned for its herd of fallow deer. Continue straight ahead across the pasture on the other side. Turn left in the next field in 250 metres. Walk up to the left-hand cluster of buildings beside **Home Farm** in 350 metres.

Fallow deer in the park

Blackrow Farm

Though the enigmatic 'Lady of Lydlinch', Margery Fitz Eleys (or Ellis) is buried here, her heart was placed in a mediaeval jar at West Parley where she owned Dudsbury Hill.

6 Here there are four paths. We take the second from the right (S), being the central public option, with the dovecote and **Stock Gaylard House** to the left. Pass **St Barnabas church** in 300

Yeatman-brand gate

metres. Beyond it lay the lost mediaeval village. Follow the drive to the main road in 400 metres.

7 Turn right (SW) and then left (SSE), in 75 metres, at **Stock Gate**. Enter **Blackrow Lane** (the **B3143** towards Kings Stag and Dorchester). Walk towards on-coming traffic. Pass **Oasis Farm** and **Blackrow Farm** - ancient and thatched - in 600 metres. In a further 500 metres we pass **Green Acres Bungalow**.

8 Turn left (E), between the next bungalows in 100 metres, into the no-through-road. Turn left (N), in 175 metres, through a Y-gate. Cross the field, towards Blackrow Farm, for 200 metres and

then bear right (NE), following the ditch and hedge for 100 metres. Go through the gate and walk the length of the next field. Pass **Hydes Withybed** in 500 metres. Continue to follow the left-hand hedgerow in the following field, for 300 metres.

9 Approach woodland at **Lower Hydes** and skirt to the left of it. Go through the gate and bear right (N) to the right-hand end of **Higher Hydes** wood - with the mast - in 200 metres. **Hydes Farm** is on the hill to its left.

10 In the following field we keep the copse to the left and go through a gate beside it, tucked into the corner of the field in 200 metres. Turn sharp right and follow the hedge

Manor Farm barn

to the next field in 150 metres. Go through the gate and bear right (NE), diagonally across the field, downhill to the far corner in 400 metres. Keep **Brake Plantation** to your left.

11 Also cross the next field to the opposite corner but this time follow the right-hand hedges. Head towards the church. Continue straight ahead in the following field, keeping the hedge to your right, to the next corner in 200 metres. Bear right in this field - towards the barns - up to the Y-gate in the skyline corner in 250 metres.

12 Turn left (N) at the road. **Manor Farm** is stone-roofed with mullioned windows.

It overlooks a triangular green. Pass **St Thomas Becket church** and return to the car-park, just beyond the 1924-built **Hooper Hall**, in 600 metres.

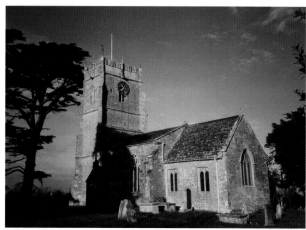

Lydlinch church

4 Fifehead Neville and Plumber Manor

A 6-mile circuit of arable and common land linked by green lanes

Level: 🥾 🥾
Length: 6 miles
Terrain: Arable fields, green lanes and a wild-wood common.
Park & start: In Fifehead Neville beside the straight section of lane in the vicinity of farm buildings, telephone kiosk and notice board.
Start ref.: ST 768 109
Postcode: DT10 2AL
Public transport: Buses from Sturminster Newton.
Websites: www.plumbermanor.co.uk
www.thedorsetpage.com

Known now for its picturesque packhorse bridge, the valley of the River Divelish once had a spectacular building, within sight of this rustic spot. Though nothing now shows on the surface, the extensive 4th-century Roman villa at Fifehead Neville was one of the largest buildings ever to stand in the Blackmore Vale. Two silver rings were found, proclaiming the owners to be wealthy Christians, as both were incised with Christ's Chi-Rho monogram and one had this symbol set beneath a winged dove with an olive branch at each side. Masonry debris included two wings of a considerable structure with column bases and an under-floor hypocaust heating system with lead piping and a rectangular plunge-bath. For opulence, there was nothing to match it until the building of the mansion at Plumber Manor in the 17th century.

Bridleways
Puxey Farm
6
Ducks Lane
Haydon Corner
Salkeld Bridge
5
Plumber Manor ■
River Divelish
7
4
Packhorse Bridge
Fifehead Neville
Deadmoor Common
8
3
10
Woodrow
Lower Fifehead Farm
9
Linton
Green Close Lane
1
Ash Tree Farm
2
500 m
Fifehead St Quintin

① Set off (E) up to the corner in 50 metres and turn right (S) at **Starlings Cottage** into **Green Close Lane**. Continue straight ahead after the houses. The green lane becomes a narrow tunnel between dense hedgerows and crosses a stream at a footbridge. The track leads to **Ash Tree Farm** at **Fifehead St Quintin** in 1,000 metres.

② Turn left (SE) down beside **Peach Farm House**, **Peach Cottages** and **Foxlair** to the junction in 200 metres. Turn left (N) to follow the railings and the **River Divelish**. Go round the corner in 250 metres and turn left into the field opposite **Lower Fifehead Farm**, through the gate to the left of the brick shed. Cross the stile in the

Lower Fifehead Farm

hedge in 125 metres and proceed along the slope to the corner of the hedge facing you in 175 metres. Enter the arable field and bear left, following the hedgerow and then the river to a footbridge, in 350 metres.

Puxey is a Dorset dialect word for a mire - so expect soggy going in places carrying the name.

Cross this and a second bridge (NNW), beside sluices and a mill-pond, and proceed straight across a paddock to gates on to the road in 175 metres.

③ Emerge at the ford. Its surface is slippery, so cross the

Packhorse bridge

mediaeval **Packhorse Bridge**. Seen as you approach the ford, we need to turn right and then left (N), through the field gate in 15 metres (on same side of road as the bridge). The site of the Roman villa is up this slope towards the electricity poles. Go through a gate in 150 metres, through riverside scrub for a further 150 metres, to a stile into an arable field. Follow the grass strip above the river to a car-park in the grounds of **Plumber Manor** in 350 metres. Turn left (W) down the drive, which is a bridleway. Take off your shoes in the porch if you indulge in an up-market pitstop.

4 Cross the humped bridge in 100 metres. The road bends to the right (NW) and brings us to a junction in 300 metres, near **Salkeld Bridge**. Cross to the gate on the other side. Bear right (N) across the field to the next gate in 200 metres. Also bear right across the following field to a hunting gate in the hedgerow in 100 metres. Head for a point to the left of lichen-covered **Puxey Farm** in 350 metres.

5 Join the farm road and pass the barns. Turn left (WSW) in **Puxey Lane** in 300 metres. Pass a couple of farmsteads and continue straight ahead (SW) at the top of the slope, in 350 metres, between the barns and **Bridleways**. Hereon **Ducks Lane** is a double-hedged track. In 700 metres it bends to the right (NW) and then, in 100 metres, we turn left (SW) into another green lane.

6 This is fringed by oaks and passes a remote farmstead. Proceed to a triangle of oaks and scrub at **Haydon Corner** in 500 metres. Fork left (SSW) into yet another green lane. This brings us to **Haydon Lane**, a wider droveway, in 450 metres. Turn right (WSW).

Plumber Manor

In 400 metres it narrows at a reed-bed and bends to the right, into an unpaved public road which can double as a stream-bed.

  Turn left (SE) at this corner, into spongy **Deadmoor Common**. This is a mixture of blackthorn, sallow, mature oaks and coarse grass, in that order of magnitude, though in places all four areas overlap into a single impenetrable habitat. The path, reasonably visible and wide, follows the left-hand boundary. Keep straight ahead, leftwards, when the track forks in a clearing in 300 metres. Birch now creeps into the tree-line and you are likely to startle the jays. Expect to disturb something in one of the wildest places in Dorset.

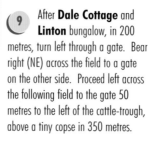 Exit in a further 700 metres, via the final strip of grass, which funnels us in 200 metres into a deep-cut track which winds and climbs to **Hambledon** bungalow and the thatched **Elm Tree Cottage** at **Woodrow** in 125 metres. Turn right (S) along the road, beside **Woodrow House**, and turn left (SE) at the junction in 25 metres. This road heads towards Fifehead Neville.

 After **Dale Cottage** and **Linton** bungalow, in 200 metres, turn left through a gate. Bear right (NE) across the field to a gate on the other side. Proceed left across the following field to the gate 50 metres to the left of the cattle-trough, above a tiny copse in 350 metres.

All Saints' church

Then bear right, to the gate beneath the pine trees in the village, in 250 metres. The view to the right is to the escarpment of the Dorset Downs in a sweep from Okeford Hill to Bulbarrow and the Dorsetshire Gap.

Turn right (S) along the track, down to the road, in 75 metres. Turn left to return to your car (or turn left at the corner in 50 metres, into the next corner in a further 50 metres, in order to visit **All Saints' church**).

5 **Sturminster Newton and Cutt Mill**

A 6-mile circuit, half of which is along the Stour riverside, between historic mills

Level: 🐾
Length: 6 miles
Terrain: Couple of slopes but otherwise gently undulating fields and meadows
Park & start: In Sturminster Newton town centre.
Start ref.: ST 786 142
Postcode: DT10 1BW
Public transport: Buses from Blandford, Dorchester and Sherborne.
Websites: www.sturminsternewton.com
www.thedorsetpage.com

This is a literary pilgrimage to key points in the lives of three Victorian authors, notably to the suitably pastoral spot where the parson-poet William Barnes was born on Bagber Common. Best known of the trio is Thomas Hardy. The third man, truly local for all his long life, was Robert Young who was also known as Rabin Hill. The principal attraction of the walk, however, is for the longest stretch of riverside path in Dorset. This runs for nearly three miles and links two very different mills at Hinton St Mary and Sturminster Newton. Both share Domesday roots and an eventful history but the first is at present in ruins, whilst the second is very much alive. Its machinery still cranks and creaks into action to produce stone-ground flour. The walk begins and ends in Sturminster Newton, the capital of the Blackmore Vale, which retains thriving hostelries.

Cutt Mill 8

Joyce's Coppice

agber ouse arm

Pentridge Farm

Manor Farm

7

River Stour

Pleak House Farm

6

Barnes Orchard

Stalbridge Lane

3 2

Sturminster Newton

Colber Bridge

1

4

Swan Inn

5

Bagber Common

500 m

White Hart Inn

Riverside

Sturminster Mill

Hardy's Riverside view

Villas (closest part of semi-detached house at end of this ridge), the home novelist Thomas Hardy and first wife Emma. Thirdly, across meadows, **Sturminster Mill** (Dorset's famous working mill).

Sturminster Mill

① Set off (W) from the cross-roads at the end of the **Market Place**, opposite **Station Road**, into **The Row**. This is the lesser option beside **Barclays Bank**, **Fern Cottage** and the **Gospel Hall**. Continue straight ahead, finally passing **Colber Cottage** in 200 metres, and proceed through a kissing gate on a downhill

path (NW) that follows a hedge and a fence.

② At the bottom, in 100 metres, we have an optional diversion leftwards (S) for 800 metres to three places of particular interest. Firstly **The Hive** (three-storey house) which was the home of Robert Young, the Victorian poet. Secondly **Riverside**

Novelist Thomas Hardy and his bride Emma Gifford made their first home in the northern of the pair of Riverside Villas where he wrote The Return of the Native *during their 'Sturminster Idyll' from July 1876 to March 1878.*

3 Our onward route is straight ahead from a stile below The Row to elegant **Colber Bridge**, an 1841-dated iron pedestrian bridge in 100 metres. Fork left (SW) on the other side along one of two paths heading to **Stalbridge Lane**. Cross the meadow to a stile to the right of a gateway in 150 metres. A narrow double-hedged track leads straight ahead and emerges on the lane in 200 metres.

Colber Bridge

1841-dated crossing

4 Continue straight ahead (WSW), uphill, through the gate on the other side. Cross into the next field through the hedge to the left in 100 metres and follow the hedgerow straight ahead. Go through the gate in the next corner, in 175 metres, and turn right to cross a stile in just 10 metres. Then follow the right-hand hedgerow straight ahead down to a bridge across the **River Divelish** in 250 metres. Proceed straight ahead (W) on the other side, up the farm road, towards Woodlands Farm.

5 In 600 metres, on reaching the trees, fork right (NW), heading towards a barn which you may have glimpsed. On coming to a cross-roads of tracks in 125 metres, turn right (N) just before the barn on former **Bagber Common**. This grassy droveway goes through triple bends to approach an oak wood in 400 metres. To the right, in a field, is **Barnes Orchard** on the site of the birthplace of Dorset poet William Barnes in 1801.

6 From the end of the wood, at the next corner in 250 metres, the bridleway bends to the left (NW) to **Pleak House** in 175 metres. Here the droveway terminates at a gate. Turn left (W), down an asphalt road, and then right (N)

Cutt Mill idyll

on joining **Bagber Lane** in 175 metres. Pass **Rushay Farm** in 100 metres and continue to **Manor Farm** and a splayed junction with **Stalbridge Lane** in 500 metres. Bear left (NW) and keep the junction and the post-box to your right.

(7) Turn right (NNE) in a further 200 metres, to pass **Bagber House Farm** and cross a bridge over the former **Somerset and Dorset Railway**. In 750 metres we approach **Lower Bagber Farm** and **Pentridge Farm**. Here the public road comes to an end. Turn left (N) between two cattle-grids, through a small gate to the left of two double gates, and continue straight ahead across the grass. There is a house and garages to the

Gutted by fire at the Millennium, Cutt Mill remains in limbo, on a rushy reach of what William Barnes called 'the clote Stour' for its yellow water-lilies.

Cutt Mill cottage

left and a barn to the right. Go through the gate in front of you, along a bridleway with a hedgerow to the left and fence to the right. Continue straight ahead (NE) across a field, keeping a hedge to your right, towards a picturesque thatched cottage and an idyllic reach of the **River Stour** in 700 metres.

(8) The path crosses a cattle track and then follows a fence which you keep to your right for the final passage across the meadows. An iron bridge on stone piers passes the mill-pond and weirs at former **Cutt Mill**. Its 18th-century buildings were on much older foundations. Go up the road between the mill and the cottage garden for 70 metres.

Barnes's clote Stour

below Blackwater Bridge and a former railway bridge in 1,600 metres.

(10) Penultimately, in a further 1,600 metres, the path passes to the right of the outskirts of Sturminster Newton and through the inner arch of the otherwise demolished **Railway Viaduct**. Cross the meadows and re-join your earlier path to the left of **Colber Bridge** in 100

(9) Turn sharp right (S), along a public path which becomes a corridor through riverside scrub, below **Joyce Cottage**. Keep the river to your right for the remainder of the walk. After the dense vegetation, the next stage is much easier as it crosses pastures beside the river-bank. Cross occasional stiles and pass the confluence of the Stour with the Divelish,

Famous Dorset parson-poet William Barnes (1801-86) was born in a cottage on Bagber Common, went to school in Sturminster Newton, and then worked as a clerk for a local solicitor.

metres Turn left (SE), uphill, to return to the town centre in 300 metres.

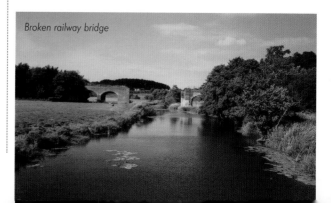

Broken railway bridge

6 **Fiddleford and Hammoon**

An 8-mile riverside and railway circuit through the heart of the Blackmore Vale

The Stour below Sturminster Newton swells into a big river. Its meadows provided Victorian engineers with an easy route for bringing the railway system from the Midlands to the South Coast. These days, however, it is as tranquil as anywhere in Dorset, and the place where you are most likely to see or hear otters as they plop into the water. Historic gems recur at regular intervals. Fiddleford not only has a fine Manor House, in the care of English Heritage, but the extensive mill buildings in one of the best settings in the county. Manston is sparse. Child Okeford is a full-size village. Hammoon oozes character, from its exquisite thatched Manor House to a tiny church which has a splendid Hamstone reredos thanks to lord of the manor Lionel Knight who came across it in a reclamation yard in 1945.

Level: ♥ ♥ ♥
Length: 8 miles.
Terrain: Low-lying pastures and occasional arable fields on thick clays.
Limitations: Muddy for most of the year and definitely off limits when the Stour floods.
Park & Start: From Fiddleford Manor car-park which is off the A357, north down Calf Close Lane, between Sturminster Newton and Shillingstone.
Start ref.: ST 801 135
Postcode: DT10 2BX
Public transport: Buses from Blandford and Sturminster Newton.
Websites: www.child-okeford.org.uk
www.opcdorset.org/hammoon

8

7

6

5

Manston House

Manor House

Hammoon

4

River Stour

9

16

10

Trailway

Downs Farmhouse

17

18

Poultry Farm

Trailway

2

1

Fiddleford Mill

19

Fiddleford Inn

11

12

Gold Hill

15

Netmead

Coneygar

13

Bere Marsh Farm

Newman's Drove

14

500 m

First admire the riverside mediaeval building in the care of English Heritage - which has the most spectacular timber roof in Dorset - but then set off the other way, via the car-park entrance. Turn left (N) and then left again (W), in 50 metres, to pass between the northern side of **Fiddleford Mill** and its ancient 'honest miller' inscription set in a panel of the farthest outbuilding in 150 metres. From here we cross

Fiddleford Manor

the **River Stour**, over the sluices and across the bridge beside the weir.

In 100 metres, in the field beyond, we turn right (NNE) and follow the river-bank to the old **Somerset and Dorset Railway** line and its restored bridge, in 300 metres. Climb the embankment beside 2007-built **Trailway Bridge** and turn left (WNW) along the cycleway. Walk to the outskirts of **Sturminster Newton** in 1,000 metres.

Here a public footpath goes under a bridge. Join it on the right-hand side of the line and bear right (NE) in the field to the corner bungalow in 100 metres. Keep all of Sturminster to your left and then bear left across a field towards agricultural

Trailway Bridge

buildings on the next rise. Cross a stile in 150 metres. Follow a double-hedged green lane (N) to the suburb of **Rixon**. Cross the farm access road in 125 metres and continue straight ahead into a corridor of paths on the other side.

Turn right (E), in 150 metres, along **Manston Road** to **Tuscans** which is the bungalow on the corner in 50 metres. Here we proceed straight ahead, downhill across a stile and along the grassy

Manston Mausoleum

Hammoon Manor and church

track immediately to the right of the garden of Tuscans. Go through the next gate and proceed to the stile and footbridge over **Chivrick's Brook** in 200 metres. We are back in the flood-plain of the Stour for the remainder of the walk.

5 There are two paths across this extensive pasture. Ours is straight ahead (ENE) towards Manston parish church. We must then cross a concrete footbridge and some stiles to the left of an oak tree in 400 metres.

Continue straight ahead towards the escarpment of Cranborne Chase with an intermittent wildlife hedge to our right. As the hedge turns towards the river, proceed straight across the pasture into the beginning of the triangular far corner of the rough grass in 1,000 metres.

6 Turn right across the stiles in the right-hand hedge midway between the river and the end of the field. On the other side bear left and keep the river to your right for the rest of the walk. In 250 metres exit from the riverside meadow through a field gate between the bungalow and barn at **Lower Farm**. This is **Manston**. Proceed to the road in 50 metres and note the 1798 datestone on the bridge over **Manston Brook**.

7 Turn right (S) across the river for a diversion along the drive to **Manston House** and its adjacent mausoleum and **St Nicholas church** in 200 metres.

8 Our onward turns right (SE) from the asphalt road into the arable field immediately beyond the drive. Head towards Hambledon Hill. Cross the stile in the far left-hand corner of the field in 500 metres. Then cross the pasture to the road in 150

Hambledon from the Stour

metres, to the left of modern **Hammoon Bridge**.

(9) Cross to the stile opposite and continue straight ahead. In 50 metres we turn right, across a stile, into the meadows. Head towards the left-hand slope of Hambledon. Just after the second ox-bow bend in the river, in 500 metres,

cross a footbridge. Up to the left, in the trees, is Fontmell Parva House. Bear right across this pasture to a gate to the left of the cattle-trough near the riverside corner.

(10) In the next field head (SE) towards the skyline gate at the corner in 200 metres. The river is to our right for 150 metres. Proceed

straight ahead across the middle of the next field. In 400 metres walk (S) beside the right-hand side of the hedgerow parallel with **Gold Hill Poultry Farm** and 100 metres to the right of its sheds. Depart from the meadows at the gate and stile in 200 metres.

(11) Turn left (E) along the green lane beyond and to the right of the poultry buildings. Turn right (S) along **Common Road** in 250 metres and enter **Child Okeford**. In 75 metres, after passing **Long**

Hammoon's name comes from 'Ham' for the meadows and 'Moon' for the de Mohun family.

Field bungalow, turn right beside the next drive, through the gate, into **Mulberry House** grounds.

12 Now turn left, over a stile, to walk along a public footpath behind the back gardens of **Gold Hill**. Next cross a stile into the pasture and follow the ditch beside the bungalow. Do the same in the next field. Emerge in **Netmead Lane**, in 300 metres, and turn right (W) along it, into the meadows. Turn left (S) in 150 metres, across a stile, and follow the hedge. Keep it to your right. In the far corner of the field, in 250 metres, we turn right (WSW) across a stile. Follow the brook for 400 metres.

13 Enter **Netmead Common** pasture and bear left (SSW),

towards the chalk quarry on Shillingstone Hill. Cross the river at the footbridge in 300 metres. The site of the **Bere Marsh Mill** is to the right. **Millham** island is a Dorset Wildlife Trust nature reserve in memory of Myrtle Cousins.

14 Bear marginally to the right on the other side to cross a footbridge in the grass and another in the hedgerow. Join **Newman's Drove** beside **Bere Marsh Farm** in 350 metres and turn right (N) along it.

15 Proceed straight ahead beside the paddocks and along the bridleway which passes an outlying barn. Then in 500 metres we continue straight ahead and pass to the right of former **Coneygar Farmhouse**.

The Somerset and Dorset Railway, in use from 1863 to 1967, carried the Pines Express from Manchester and Birmingham to the seaside at Bournemouth West station.

Also continue straight ahead in the field and keep the riverside scrub to your right. Our path, up and over the rise, passes to the left of **Diggers Copse** and **Ham Down Copse** in 500 metres. Proceed straight ahead across the following field and pass to the left of the next coppice in 300 metres. Then follow a hedge, to our left, and leave this field at the second of two gates in the corner.

16 In 1,000 metres the hedge brings us to **Downs**

Farmhouse. Here the bridleway becomes a double-hedged lane for the final 300 metres into **Hammoon** village. The cross-roads, where we are to turn left (SW) is replete with the stump of a mediaeval cross. For a short but rewarding diversion continue straight ahead to visit **St Mary's church** and the exquisite thatched **Manor Farm**.

 Leave the village, in 200 metres, between **Victory Cottages** and **Rambler Cottages** (named for roses rather than walkers). In a further 400 metres turn right (W) into a farm track and then immediately left (S) through the bridleway gate. Follow the hedgerow headland beside two arable fields. Turn right (NW), in 600 metres, on reaching

Music at Fiddleford Inn

the **Trailway** beside the road, to follow the track-bed of the old railway. Follow it for 900 metres.

 Turn left (S), along a grassy public path, and follow the hedge to the corner in 225 metres.

The Cross

Then follow the same hedge to the right (E) to the road in 100 metres. Turn left (S) into the hamlet of **Fiddleford** and the **Fiddleford Inn** in 400 metres (take off your shoes in the porch).

 Turn around on leaving, without joining the main road, and fork left (N) in 75 metres, after **Willow Tree Cottage**, into an asphalt road which becomes a narrow green lane after passing **Manor Farmhouse**, to squeeze between a stream and the former frontages of the cottages. Turn left on reaching the lane after the beech hedge in 350 metres and then left at the junction in 150 metres to return to the car-park on your right.

7 Okeford Fitzpaine and Shillingstone

Green lanes and primeval woods on an undulating 6-mile circuit

Few villages are so blessed with visible history at multiple levels. In places the streets of Okeford Fitzpaine have been worn into hollow ways. Raised pavements and railings thread beneath half-timbered walls, often banded with mixtures of brick, flint and quarried ashlar. Miscellaneous survivals include the pound, the stump of a wayside cross, the door of the village lock-up, and a Victorian fire-engine and bier in a roadside shed. Beside it is a green telephone kiosk painted that colour, it is said, because lord of the manor Captain George Pitt-Rivers had an aversion to red (being synonymous with communism). He sold a third of the village, mostly to its tenants, to cheers in the auction room in 1966. Dorset Wildlife Trust manages 67 acres of Piddles Wood as a nature reserve.

Level: 🥾 🥾
Length: 6 miles
Terrain: Variable vegetation which can be wild and tangled in places.
Park & start: In Back Lane, beside St Andrew's church, in Okeford Fitzpaine.
Postcode: DT11 0RD
Public transport: Buses from Blandford and Sturminster Newton.
Websites:
www.okeford-fitzpaine.org.uk
www.shillingstone.info

Map labels:

Piddles Wood
4
5
Angers Corner
Lodge Farm
6
Banbury Cross
Angers Farm
Conygar Coppice
3
The Knapps
7
Fiddleford Mushrooms
Darknoll Farm
8
Lanchards
Darknoll Lane
Little Lane
9
Red House
Royal Oak
2
Duck Street
10
1
11 Shillingstone House
Okeford Fitzpaine
Pound Lane
12
500 m

St Lo House

Robert Fitzpaine fought with the barons and seized the royal seal from Henry III at the Battle of Lewes on 14 May 1264.

beside the entrance to **Darknoll Farm** in 750 metres. Up the slope, in a further 750 metres, you emerge into the wide drive beside **Fiddleford Mushrooms**.

① Head into the centre of the village (NW), uphill beside **St Lo House**, and bear right beside **Ye Olde Bell Stores** in 175 metres. Pass the 1873-dated **Primary School**. Turn left in 50 metres, beside **Royal Oak Inn**, along **Lower Street**. Pass historic **Yeatmans**, **Mary Gardens** and 1830-dated **Chapel Cottage** in 300 metres.

② Turn right (N), in 150 metres, into **Darknoll Lane**. The asphalt road becomes a green lane

St Andrew's church

Piddles Wood

③ Continue straight ahead at **Banbury Cross**. Follow the lane uphill, beside **Piddles Wood**, for 600 metres.

④ Turn right into the woodland car-park, opposite a barn, near the top of the hill. Bear right (E), through the gate, down along the main track. Continue straight ahead (NE) at a turning circle and proceed to the Dorset Wildlife Trust sign in

600 metres. Here we turn right (E), off the forest road, towards Angers Farm. Turn right (SE) at the next junction of paths, in 500 metres, towards Angers Lane.

⑤ Go down into to the gates into the field above the farm in 150 metres. Bear left (SW) to the next gate in 10 metres. Cross the corner of the paddock to the following

Piddles Wood, mainly of oak under-grown with coppiced hazel since Saxon times, has primeval origins as shown by wild service trees which were never planted for forestry.

gate in 35 metres. Bear right across the following pasture to a gate in 100 metres. Then cross the lower paddock

Half-timbered cottages

Conygar Coppice

into the former **Landfill Site**. Follow the asphalt road, beside what is currently a travellers' camp, down to the corner in **Conygar Coppice** in 275 metres. Turn right into the trees and then follow the main track up and round to the left (SE) over the middle of the higher ground. Take the centre option, ahead and downhill, from a woodland cross-roads in 275 metres. Exit through a bridleway gate in 150 metres. Follow the hedgerow beside two arable fields with Hambledon Hill to the left and Shillingstone Hill chalk quarry to the right.

to the gates to the left of **Lodge Farm**, in 100 metres. Bear right down across the next field, through a gate in 150 metres, and then left to a gate near the corner, beneath an oak tree in a further 150 metres.

6 Turn left (E) along the road, passing **Angers Farm**, to Angers Corner in 400 metres. Turn right along the main road for 40 metres and then right (SE), into a gap in the dense hedgerow, and climb to a stile. Follow the hedge uphill to a stile and gate at **The Knapps** in 500 metres.

7 Turn right (S) along **Castle Lane** for 125 metres. Turn left (E) through the right-hand gate

8 Cross **Little Lane** at the gates in 300 metres. Cross the field to a gate and stile to the right of the power line in 400 metres. Cross **Cookwell Brook** and the

Shillingstone Hill

The mediaeval Shelin or Eskilling family gave their name to the linear village of Shillingstone.

following stile. Bear left to the far corner of the pasture in 175 metres. Continue across the next pasture to the gate and stile beside the road at **Lanchards** in 100 metres.

9 Turn left and then right into **Lanchards Lane**. Turn left from the corner after the **Red House** in 150 metres. Walk between the paddocks. Cross the drive in 100 metres, to a stile between the gates, and proceed to the next stile in 100 metres. A ferny track under the trees leads to the drive approaching **Shillingstone House** in 50 metres.

10 Turn right (SW) to the bend in the drive in 125 metres. Continue straight ahead, keeping the laurel hedge to your left, and proceed through the vegetation to a gate and steps in 250 metres.

11 Climb the stile on the other side of the road. Cross the field to a stile and iron footbridge, over the brook, in the far left-hand corner in 250 metres. Enter the next field and bear right (W) into another pasture in 50 metres. Cross double stiles in the hedgerow ahead in 100 metres. Follow the next hedgerow to the rounded corner in 250 metres. Turn right and then immediately left to the corner

Primitive Methodist chapel

Okeford Fitzpaine is – or was – known by the sobriquet 'Fippenny Ockford' which provided the title for Tom Graham's book about the parish in the 1950s.

of this adjacent field in 100 metres. Cross the stile and footbridge. Turn left (S) through the scrub to an unpaved road in 150 metres.

12 Turn right (W) along **Pound Lane**. Proceed straight ahead at the cross-roads of tracks in 150 metres. Pass **Church Farm** and the 1859-dated **Primitive Methodist chapel** in 600 metres. From here the asphalt road rises to **Back Lane**, in 100 metres, with the church beside the junction.

8 Hambledon and Hod

Two major Iron Age hill-forts on a fascinating 6-mile circuit

'The spectacular natural setting of Hambledon Hill,' English Nature proclaims, 'has attracted man since

Neolithic times. The massive hill-fort is of later Iron Age origin. This is one of the few substantial flower-rich downlands left in Dorset. See attractive plants and animals such as early gentian, meadow saxifrage and Adonis blue butterflies.' Views from Hambledon Hill are into the Blackmore Vale, where the River Stour heads for a gap through the Dorset Downs, and to Cranborne Chase. Hod Hill has both Iron Age and Roman forts. Child Okeford, remembered from childhood as the

Level: 🐾 🐾 🐾
Length: 6 miles
Terrain: Hilly with one particularly precipitous descent where you may slip and slide, though there are trees to grab.
Park & start: In Child Okeford village.
Start ref.: ST 835 127
Postcode: DT11 8ED
Public transport: Buses from Blandford and Shaftesbury.
Websites: www.dorsetaonb.org.uk
www.imagesofdorset.org.uk

home of television puppets Sooty and Sweep, has numerous gentrified 18th-century cottages. These are outranked by the truly Old House with a mix of quality farmhouse architecture.

1 Set off (N) from the **Cross** beside the drive to **St Nicholas church**, opposite the 18th-century **Baker Arms** downhill for 50 metres to the next road junction. Turn right into **Upper Street,** towards Iwerne Minster and Shaftesbury, and pass **Barley House** and **Foxdale Pottery**. In 750 metres, on the corner just after **Oasis Health Centre**, turn right (NE) opposite its beech hedge into a double-hedged green lane.

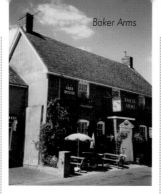
Baker Arms

2 **Sandy Lane** passes **Chalkpit Farm** and becomes a ferny hollow way, through a tunnel of holly. At the top end, in 150 metres, enter an arable field and proceed straight ahead (E) across it, following the power cables. Approach **Shroton Lines**. Turn right (SSW) in 250 metres and follow the fence uphill to the gate, to enter the **National Nature Reserve**, in 200 metres.

3 Climb the steep slope of **Hambledon Hill** and turn left (S) along the summit. The hog's back rises in 500 metres into a long barrow communal burial mound

St Nicholas church

Shroton Lines

Hambledon hill-fort

multiple ditches. The defenders practised slingstone warfare until the Roman invasion of AD 43 and its sequel in which their noble colleagues on Hod Hill were vanquished.

(4) Beyond these ramparts we go back in time to 3500 BC and the peoples who built the long barrow. In 150 metres, cross the lesser traces of their causewayed camp compound, its outer defences being under

dating from 3000 BC. Beyond it in 100 metres is a substantial cross-dyke extending over the hill which formed part of the original outer defences of the hill-fort before it was strengthened and extended. A total of 207 hut platforms, scattered across 31 acres

inside the ramparts, have been counted from a combination of archaeological fieldwork and aerial photography. Many of them are down to our right. In another 300 metres we depart (SE) through the great Iron Age entrenchments which had palisaded banks and

Causewayed camp trig-point

the later hill-fort. As for the homestead, its earthworks were ploughed up with Government encouragement in the agricultural madness of the 1960s, to prevent it being 'damaged by rabbits'. Having passed the Ordnance Survey triangulation in another 50 metres we are at the centre of the Neolithic camp. Ahead, in 250 metres, is **Coombe Wood**.

 For 800 metres our path skirts above and around the south-ern edge of the wood. Then turn right (S) towards **Keeper's Lodge** and the road in 500 metres. Extending down to the right are the spooky groves of Dorset's only yew wood.

 Cross the road, bearing to the right, to the gate that is virtually opposite. Here we climb the grassy slope, bearing right (SSW), beside and above **Leigh Wood**. The yew wood is now on the opposite hillside. Enter National Trust land at

Hod Hill has a unique double set of fortifications with an invasion-period Roman fort built in the corner of its earlier Iron Age ramparts.

Hod Hill fort in 400 metres. The Iron Age earthworks are roughly square with sides 650 metres in length. Ideally make the time to give it a proper explore. Leftwards in the middle of the hill is the site of the chieftain's hut excavated by Sir Ian Richmond in 1951, which had been torched by burning ballista-bolts fired by Roman artillery machines from outside the ramparts. Vespasian's 2nd Legion Augusta conquered the hill and built a fort inside the top right-hand corner. Freak acoustics

Hod Hill

mean that you can sometimes hear the conversations of walkers from the other side of the valley which is a phenomenon usually associated with mountainous terrain.

(7) Our onward route (S) is down from the Roman fort to the lower corner, above the river, in 400 metres. Here we drop down into a dip and bear left (SW) beside an extension bank that forms a triangular addition down from the

Barley House, a Victorian temperance café and hotel - nicknamed 'The Chocolate House' - became the main base of Child Okeford and Iwerne Minister Co-Operative Society.

Roman fort corner

main hill-fort. Exit from National Trust land at the far end of the outwork in 100 metres. Drop down through the steep and flinty wood, clinging to the trees if necessary and keeping your feet out of badger holes, for a demanding 150 metres down to **Hod Drove**.

(8) Turn right (N) with the **River Stour** to your left for 800 metres. Then bear right (NE) through

the wild wood for 250 metres. On coming out of **Hod Wood** we emerge on an asphalt road beside a small car-park, opposite a bank which conceals an 18th-century ice-house.

(9) Our onward route is left (W) to the drive of **Hanford House** in 800 metres. Turn left to approach the building where Sir Arthur Sullivan composed *Onward Christian Soldiers* and titled it *St*

51

Gertrude in gratitude to hostess Miss Gertrude Clay-Ker-Seymer. Turn right (N) in 125 metres along the drive opposite the entrance to the house, which is now a girls' school, and then turn left (NW) in 20 metres along a public footpath in a narrow corridor between garden hedges.

(10) In 300 metres we cross a junction of farm tracks to the gate facing us. Ignore the gate into the woods. Our path is straight ahead (W) into the field with the wood to

Child Okeford parish church, rebuilt in 1879, apart from its Tudor tower, was the venue for the first performance of Sir Arthur Sullivan's hymn Onward Christian Soldiers in 1871.

the right. In the corner, in 225 metres, turn right (N) across a stile. Cross the centre of the field, for 400 metres, with **Fox Ditch Coppice** across to the left and **Little Hanford Villa** to the right. Also keep the next cluster of buildings to your right. On reaching the farm road, turn left (SW), downhill to the hedges in 250 metres.

(11) Turn right (N) along a dirt-surfaced bridleway to **Melway Farm** in 600 metres. Continue straight ahead along the tarred road into **Child Okeford** village. In 400 metres we proceed straight ahead at the cross-roads. **Pilgrim's Farm** to the right was the home of Harry Corbett - plus Sooty and Sweep - who had modern

Pilgrim's Farm

taste when it came to farmhouse renovation.

(12) Cross a stile into the path sandwiched between garden fences and also follow it straight ahead beyond the housing estate cul-de-sac in 150 metres. In 100 metres, at the end of the following cul-de-sac, we turn right (E) into another path to the left of No. 21. It emerges in the main street in 50 metres where we turn left (N), to return to the **Baker Arms** in 150 metres.

9 **Hazelbury Bryan and Mappowder**

A pastoral 6-mile circuit of lowland fields, lanes, lakes and small woods

Ordinary decent countryside at the heart of the Blackmore Vale includes two typical villages, scattered farms and the occasional mansions both ancient and modern. There is no public house en route but the Hazelbury Bryan starting point is up the street from the Antelope Inn which is on the Hardy Way.

Its appearance is in *Tess of the d'Urbervilles* when the heroine passes through Nuttlebury (Hazelbury Bryan) on her return to Marlott (Marnhull) from Abbot's Cernel (Cerne Abbas). In a Hardyesque echo, former natives of

Level: 🥾 🥾
Length: 6 miles.
Terrain: Variable, from grass to mud.
Park & start: In the wide street at Wonston opposite the main range of thatch in Hazelbury Bryan village.
Postcode: DT10 2EE
Public transport: Buses from Blandford, Dorchester and Sturminster Newton.
Websites:
www.hazelburybryan.com
www.opcdorset.org.uk/mappowder

Hazelbury such as farmer Tom Bunter always called it 'Hazzle-burr' in broad Dorset dialect. Mappowder provided a safe haven for members of the literary Powys family, to escape the war.

Map labels:
Povert Bridge Farm
Hazelbury Bryan 1
Coney Lane 2 3
Drum Lane School 4 Manor Farm
Droop Farm
Boywood Farm
Wonston
11 12
Thickthorn Lane 5
Dairy House Farm
Stivvicks Bridge 6
Nut Bloom Cottage
Stoke Lane
10 Styles Farm Bungalow
Taylor's Lane 7
9
Mappowder Mappowder Court 8
500 m

Hazelbury almshouse and church

St Mary and St James's church

 Set off (NE) along **Drum Lane**, beside thatched **Nuttlebury,** and pass **Green-acres**, **Tea Kettle House**, **Mead Cottage** and **The Meadow**. In 200 metres the road becomes a public path into the fields. Follow the right-hand hedgerow for 300 metres.

② Turn right (ENE) on reaching narrow **Coney Lane**. Turn right (SE) at the road in 400 metres.

③ Turn left in 60 metres, into the field, and bear right downhill for 100 metres. Go through a gate in the hedge facing you. Proceed straight ahead beside the next hedgerow, through a gate in 350 metres, and continue to the road beside the 2004-dated **Primary School** in 200 metres.

④ Cross the road to the **Almshouse** and **St Mary and St James's church**. Go up the church path to a gate beside the church porch where our public path enters a private garden. Its way-marked course is to the right of the

Wonston cottages

Stoke Lane lake

smaller pond to **Manor Farm** drive in 75 metres. Grass snakes are harmless, by the way, should you be lucky enough to see them. Turn right (SW) and proceed to the double gates on to the road in 100 metres. Turn left (SE) and pass **Droop Farm**. Bear right (SW) at the bend in 400 metres.

5 **Thickthorn Lane** brings us to **Park Gates** junction in 800 metres. Turn right (NW) beside **Nut Bloom Cottage** and then left (SW), before the next building, in 50

The stone-roofed former Almshouse at Hazelbury Bryan, restored in 1939, carries the text 'Peace be within thy walls'.

metres. This overgrown green lane leads straight into the fields in 350 metres. Follow the hedgerow straight ahead and go through the bridleway gate in 100 metres. Cross the next pasture to the gate and footbridge in the left-hand corner in 225 metres. Continue straight ahead to the next hedgerow in 150 metres.

6 Cross the stream here, at wooden **Stivvick's Bridge**, and turn left (SE) to a gate on to the road in 225 metres. Proceed straight ahead along **Stoke Lane**. Turn right (E) through the gate in 250 metres. Bear right to the right-hand gate in the corner of the pasture in 200 metres. Keep the gallops to your left and the fishing lakes to the right.

Go through a gate in 300 metres and a second gate on to the road in a further 20 metres.

7 Turn left (SW) to the corner in 400 metres. Turn left (SE), passing **Ivy Cottage**, to the stone-roofed barn at **Mappowder Court Farm** in 350 metres. Bear right (S) to pass the front garden of 1745-rebuilt **Mapperton Court** and continue to the end of the road in 150 metres.

8 Turn right (W) up a paved bridleway to the road at **Town's Knap** in 350 metres. Turn right (N) uphill into **Mappowder** and visit the **church of St Peter and St Paul**, around the corner in 400 metres. The Powys burials are towards the road. Leave by the gate

Mappowder Court

beside the table-tomb of 1640 to Roger Trewe the Elder. Turn left (NW) beside **Newleaze Lodge** which was novelist Theodore Francis Powys's last home. Walk down to the **Old Post House** at the corner in 250 metres.

9 Turn left into the track between the telephone kiosk and **Styles Farm Bungalow**, to a gate in 75 metres. There are two paths in this field. Ours follows the right-hand fence to a stile in 125 metres. Bear right (NNW), following the power cables, up to a gate to the

left of the house in 350 metres. Cross **Taylor's Lane** and turn immediately left (WNW) across a stile beside the gate. Walk across this field to the far corner, down between two oak trees, in 400 metres. Cross the stile and follow the hedge straight ahead to a gate in 200 metres.

10 Turn right (NNE) into this field and head for the right-hand side of **Short Wood** in 350 metres. Go through the gate beside it (N) in 50 metres and continue straight ahead to a hunting gate in the hedge in 200

Hazelbury Bryan church has a 12th-century font and painted royal arms, for George I, dated 1715.

metres. Turn right (NNE) for 250 metres and then turn right (E) through a gate. Turn left (NE) through the next gate, in 100 metres, and walk up and over the rounded hill. Bear right from the top, heading to the left of **Dairy House Farm**, with the houses of Hazelbury Bryan strung along the hill-top beyond. Go through the gate near the far corner in 500 metres.

Bust of T. F. Powys in Dorset County Museum

(11) Cross the field to the hedge on the other side and turn right (ENE) beside **Boywood Farm**. Proceed beside the hedge, to a stile on to the road, to the left of the house. Turn right (S) and then left through the field gate at **Povert Bridge Farm** in 25 metres. Turn right and go through the next gate in 25 metres. Then bear left (SE) for 250 metres.

(12) Turn left (NE) across the stile beside the left-hand of the two gates. Cross the footbridge in 75 metres. Turn right beside the stream, go under the power cables, and walk up the slope to a stile in the hedge in 175 metres. Continue straight ahead, uphill, to the stile to the right of house in 150 metres. Head for the

Powys family graves

gate and stile beside the trees between the houses in 200 metres. Pass **Orchard Farmhouse** and **Wessex Cottage** on return to **Wonston** in 150 metres.

The last home of Theodore Francis Powys (1875-1953), author of Mr Weston's Good Wine, was in the Lodge beside the churchyard at Mappowder where he is buried.

10 **Bulbarrow and Woolland**

A 5-mile circuit half in the vale and half looking down on it

This walk drops into the Blackmore Vale from the 900-feet chalk escarpment of Bulbarrow Hill. The hilltop just about touches the iconic spot-height but the AA topograph (claiming '901 feet') has been erected on the 875-feet contour. What there can be no doubt about is that this is 'a damn fine view' as one of its farmers described it. Initially breathtaking, it widens to include a catalogue of landmarks. Distant heights, from left to right, are the Blackdown Hills (40 miles away), Quantock Hills (45 miles), Glastonbury Tor (27 miles), King Alfred's Tower (18 miles) and Shaftesbury (12 miles). The tallest object is the Mendip television transmitter, standing 1,001 feet at 994 feet above sea level in the Mendip Hills (20 miles). Rawlsbury Camp, on the adjacent spur was the largest Iron Age hill-fort in central Dorset. Bulbarrow had a

Level: 🥾 🥾 🥾
Length: 5 miles
Terrain: Several prolonged climbs across the spring-line.
Park & start: In the viewpoint car-park on top of Bulbarrow Hill, above Stoke Wake, Woolland and Ibberton.
Start ref.: ST 783 059
Postcode: DT11 0HQ
Public transport: None.
Websites:
www.maps.google.co.uk
www.megalithic.co.uk

invasion beacon during the Napoleonic Wars, an RAF bomber navigation station during the Second World War, and United States Air Force communications masts through the Cold War.

Map

Woolland 10
8 9
Old Rectory — Hill Farm — Chitcombe Farm 11 12
Stoke Wake 5 — 6 — 7
4 — Manor Farm
Woolland Hill
2
1 **Bulbarrow Hill**
Inners Bottom — Rawlsbury Camp — masts
3
500 m

Bulbarrow view

Dorset's highest point

(1) Set off (W) to the staggered cross-roads in 100 metres and fork right along the Stoke Wake option, with masts to your left and North Dorset district council's **Woolland Hill** nature reserve along the hillside to the right. Continue straight ahead at the next junction in 800 metres. Fork left at the following junction in 175 metres.

(2) Turn left at the gate in 200 metres. Then bear right and follow the ancient grass trackway into

Rawlsbury Camp

the Iron Age defences of **Rawlsbury Camp** hill-fort in 300 metres. Bear left (SW), following the inner bank, and go through a gate in 50 metres. Proceed beside the left-hand entrenchments for 150 metres. Then descend through the earthworks on to a spur of downland above a collection of little lakes. Go through the hedge 150 metres beyond the fort (to the left of the beech wood). Descend the slope to a gate in the kink in the hedge on the opposite side of the field in 200 metres.

Stoke Wake

(3) Do not go through this gate. Leave the Wessex Ridgeway at this point. Stay in this field and turn right (N) to another gate in 100 metres. Continue straight ahead, down and then across **Skinner's**

Bottom to the gate on the other side in 200 metres, to the left of the wood. Bear left (NW) to climb the ridge, diagonally, to the copse on the skyline in 200 metres. Turn right (NNE) on reaching the trees and keep the wood to your left. In the corner of the field in 175 metres we are funnelled into the hazel coppice. Proceed (NNW) down to the road in 200 metres.

(4) Turn left (N) down into the tiny village of **Stoke Wake** at the foot of the hill. After the barn

The mock-Gothic manor at Woolland House was demolished in 1962 and the present house comprises its stables and outbuildings.

and stables, in 200 metres, pass the entrance to **Manor Farm**. Turn right in 20 metres into the double driveways to the **Old Rectory**. Fork right (E) and walk down to the bend in the drive to the house in 150 metres. Turn right (S) between beech trees, cross a trickle of a stream, and enter the churchyard of **All Saints' church** in 12 metres.

Mappowder Manor

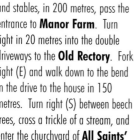

Hedgerow scabious

5 Turn left (E) and descend steps in 10 metres. Proceed straight ahead for 100 metres, after a row of conifers, and then bear right

Woolland church, rebuilt by architect Gilbert Scott in 1855, is said to be the third church shadowed by the ancient multi-trunked yew tree which has a girth of 29 feet.

(SE) across parkland, down to a footbridge across the stream in 50 metres. Head uphill through the trees to a gate and stile in 75 metres.

6 Turn left (NE), uphill, and keep the hedge to your left. In 250 metres, at the corner of the field, go through an iron kissing gate and descend through the trees to the next kissing gate, beside the stream in 50 metres. Follow the hedge in the field, uphill, for 100 metres. Pass gates as you go over the brow of the

Great yew

hill and drop down to another kissing gate in 40 metres.

7 Continue straight ahead (E) for 100 metres, through an ornamental glade with apple and walnut trees, to the next kissing gate. Proceed for 15 metres to a cottage at **Hill Farm**. Turn left (NNE) along the track and pass the Victorian Gothic farmhouse and barns. The drive, which becomes an asphalt road, leads to 1902-built **Ivy Cottages** and a road junction in 500 metres.

8 Turn left and then follow the road around to the right (E) into **Woolland**. In the next 200 metres, pass **Hillside**, **Springhill**, **Keeper's Cottage**, **Manor House**, **Old School House** and

Woolland church (no known dedication) with its great spreading yew. Next we pass **Woolland House**, which was Dame Elisabeth Frink's home, and come to a left-hand bend in 175 metres.

(9) Turn right (SE) here, on to a track into a wood, but then turn left in 10 metres, through a kissing gate. Bear right (ESE) diagonally across the field - towards the farm - and go through the hedge at a sycamore tree in 250 metres. Bear left,

Elisabeth Frink's grave

downhill, to the gates to the right of a bungalow in 150 metres. Cross the parking area to the road in 20 metres.

(10) Turn right (SE) and pass the flint and brick of **Chitcombe Farm** to proceed straight ahead between its stables in 150 metres. You come to a stream in the dip in 50 metres. In a further 10 metres the road forks three ways.

(11) Take the centre option which is a double-hedged track up the hill. In 150 metres you come to three more choices and again take the centre one (S). This becomes an ancient hollow way that bends to the left (SE) on the middle section of the **Bulbarrow** ascent in 200 metres. Then pass above the corner of an old field bound-

Graves at Stoke Wake include a 1977 memorial to 'Patron of the Living' Frank Notley Kent who erected a hilltop cross at Rawlsbury and is accompanied by 'Sally and Hector, with Master. Ever faithful, Ever sure.'

ary, with some big trees, and press on uphill - through the gorse - to a hunting gate in 400 metres.

(12) Stop and do not go through it. Instead turn right (S) up another bridleway, staying inside the open downland. The path gradually converges with the road and joins it at a gate in 400 metres. Turn right (SW) to return to the parking strip in 900 metres.